BACKGAMMON

BACKGAMMON

*An easy-to-follow illustrated guide to
playing this classic game of strategy*

JON TREMAINE

About the Author

Jon Tremaine, a professional magician for over thirty years, was introduced to backgammon while performing his act in Swaziland. He has since played the game in a multitude of countries around the world, and lectures about and teaches backgammon to groups throughout the UK. He is the author of *The Amazing Book of Backgammon* (1995), and many other books on subjects as diverse as magic, origami, divination and prediction, and dream interpretation.

This is a Parragon Book
This edition published in 2000

Parragon
Queen Street House
4 Queen Street
Bath BA1 1HE, UK

Copyright © Parragon 1999

Designed, packaged and produced by
Stonecastle Graphics Limited

ISBN 0-75253-212-X

Editor: Philip de Ste. Croix
Photographer: Andrew Dee
Hand model: Silvia Bucher

Manufactured in China

The Doubling Cube

Most backgammon sets are supplied with a doubling cube that is used to increase the stakes during the course of play. Pages 52–55 explain the use of the doubling cube in detail. On occasions, you may come across a set that lacks a doubling cube. In such circumstances it is quite simple to manufacture your own. First find a spare die – the larger, the better – and stick blank paper labels to each of the six faces. Then inscribe one of the following numbers onto each face of the die: 2, 4, 8, 16, 32, 64. The result: a perfectly satisfactory doubling cube. Let battle commence!

Contents

Introducing Backgammon 6
The Object of the Game 8
Rolling Doubles, Hitting Blots 10
Bearing Off 12
Starting the Game 14
The 36 Possible Throws 16
General Strategy 18
The Opening Moves 20
Replies to the Opening Moves 28
The Importance of Primes 32
Playing Against a Prime 34
The Running Game 36
Calculating Your Position 38
The Back Game 40
Bearing Off 44
High or Low – First or Last 46
Which One First? 48
The Odds 50
The Doubling Cube 52
General Doubling Advice 56
Playing Etiquette 58
The Official Rules of Backgammon 60
Chouette 64

Introducing Backgammon

◎

WHEN YOU are playing backgammon, life is always unpredictable. Victory can be snatched from you at the very last moment and, likewise, disaster is sometimes avoided even when you seem to be firmly gripped within the jaws of defeat. No wonder backgammon has been described as the cruellest game in the world.

It is a comparatively easy game to learn to play, but an extremely difficult game to learn to play well. It combines the excitement of chance with the cool calculation of odds and strategy. It is, quite simply, unadulterated war!

A 24-inch backgammon set used in tournament play and (behind) an 18-inch travelling set.

Backgammon is a game for two people. It is played on a strange-looking board that looks rather like an opened attaché case. Both players have 15 men, two dice and a dice shaker. There is also a doubling cube. This is like a large die, the sides of which are numbered 2, 4, 8, 16, 32 and 64. The doubling cube is used to increase the stakes of the game during the course of play. Its use is explained on pages 52-55.

The players are known as "Black" and "White" according to the colour of the pieces with which they respectively play. **In this book you will always play as White.**

The players sit on opposite sides of the board. The board is marked out with 24 pointers. The 30 pieces are known as **men** There are 15 black and 15 white men. To begin the game they are set up as shown (**A**).

The raised centre area of the board that effectively divides the set into two is called the bar. The board is thought of as having four quarters or "tables". Each player has an inner and an outer table and each table has six pointers or points.

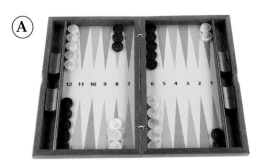

(A)

BLACK'S OUTER TABLE	BLACK'S INNER TABLE
12 11 10 9 8 7	6 5 4 3 2 1
WHITE'S OUTER TABLE	WHITE'S INNER TABLE

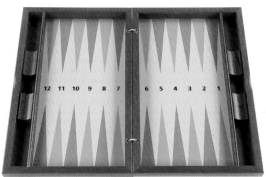

(B)

Those in the inner table are numbered 1-6 and the points in the outer table are numbered 7-12 (**B**). So White's 12 points are known as: (inner table) W1, W2, W3, W4, W5, W6; (outer table) W7, W8, W9, W10, W11 and W12. Black's points are correspondingly known as B1, B2, B3, B4, B5, B6, B7, B8, B9, B10, B11 and B12 (**C**). These numbers do not appear on your backgammon board. They are used purely to assist clarity of notation in this book so that you

will be able to follow the moves of the men exactly throughout each section.

(C)

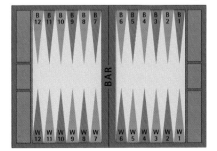

The Object of the Game

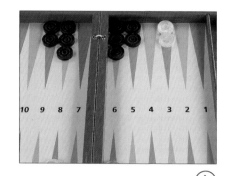

EACH PLAYER moves his men, according to the throw of his two dice, round the board and into his own inner table. Once all 15 of his men are there, he is allowed to begin to remove them from the board completely, also as determined by the throws of his dice. The first player to remove all of his men wins the game. However, it's not as simple as it sounds. Your opponent is, of course, trying to impede your progress around the board, and one of the ways he can do this is by using his own men to set up blockades or **blocked points**.

BLOCKED POINTS

Any point on which two or more men are positioned is called a blocked point (**A**). You cannot stop on a point that is "blocked" by your opponent's men. Six blocked points in a row are called a **prime** (see also pages 32-33). If you manage to create a prime, your opponent's men will be trapped behind it, unable to hop over it until such time as you break up the prime. Three, four or five blocked points in a row are called a **semi-prime**.

MOVING

Seen from White's point of view, White moves in an anti-clockwise direction around the board, while Black moves in a clockwise direction. (**B**). A player moves his men the same number of points as his thrown dice indicate. Example: Suppose you rolled 4-2. You may move one man four places and another man two places. Alternatively, you could move one man four places and the same man a further two places (**C**). Each half of your roll must end on a point that is either:

(a) "open" with no men on it
(b) has one or more of your own men already on it

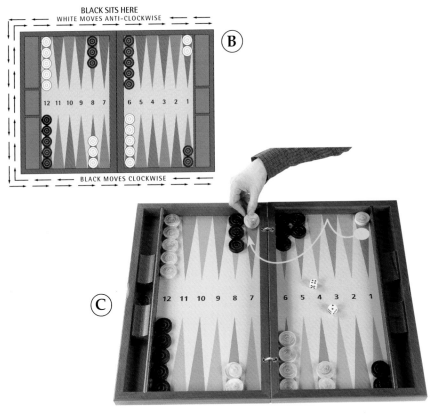

(c) has only one of your opponent's men on it – in other words, not a blocked point

You start your count from the point adjacent to the one from which you are moving. You pass over and count every point whether there are men on it or not.

Always think of your roll as two separate moves rather than combining the totals of the dice to make a single number. The 4-2 roll for example, can be played as a 4 move and then a 2 move or as a 2 move followed by a 4 move. **It is not an 6 move.** A player **must** use both numbers of each roll whenever possible.

Rolling Doubles, Hitting Blots

WHEN A player rolls the same number on each die he is permitted to play the roll **twice**. For example, if you rolled 4-4, you may move:

a) One man 16 places (4+4+4+4=16)
b) Two men 8 places (8+8=16)
c) Four men 4 places each (4+4+4+4=16)
d) One man 12 places and a second man 4 places (12+4=16).

BLOTS, HITTING AND RE-ENTERING
A single man on a point is called a **blot** (**A**). A blot is vulnerable and can be "hit" by your opponent if he lands on it. The man that is hit is lifted from the board and placed on the bar. It has to be re-entered in your opponent's inner table on any open point before you can make any other move. Therefore, for example, if your opponent (Black) has successfully blocked his B6 and B5 points, you (White) have to roll a 1, 2, 3 or 4 with your dice before your man is allowed to re-enter from the bar (**B**).

Say you roll 5-1. You would re-enter your man on B1 (**C**) and then move a different man five places. If you rolled 3-4, you could either re-enter on B3 and then move the 4 or re-enter on B4 and move the 3 elsewhere. If, however you rolled 6-5, 5-5 or 5-6 you would be unable to re-enter and would forfeit your turn because your man on the bar **must** be re-entered before you are permitted to execute any other move.

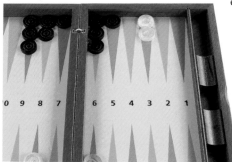

(A)

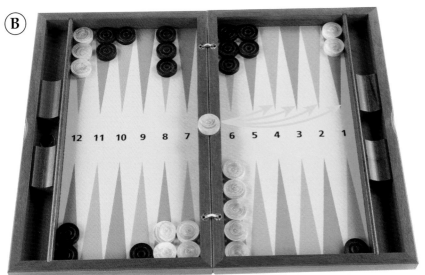

(B)

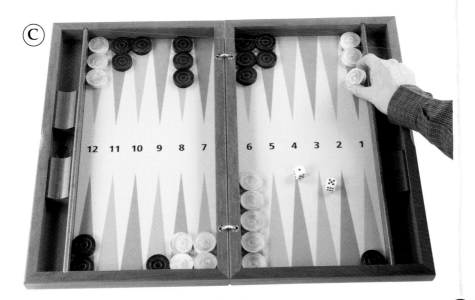

(C)

Bearing Off

ONCE ALL 15 of your men are safely inside your inner table you begin "**bearing**" them off, i.e. removing them completely from the board. The inner table is numbered 1 to 6 and you bear off men corresponding to the numbers thrown on your dice. Supposing you (White) roll 4-2, you remove one man from your W4 point and one man from your W2 point. If you were lucky enough to roll 4-4 you would remove four men from your W4 point (assuming you had four men positioned there).

If you have no men on the bearing-off point indicated by your dice, the move must be made within your inner table. For example if you throw 4-1 and you have an open W4 point, you would remove one man from W1 for the 1 and then move one man four places from W6 to W2 (**A**).

If by bearing off you risk leaving a vulnerable blot, you may instead make an alternative move within your inner table if it is possible to do so. If it is not possible, then the man must be removed from the board whether you like it or not!

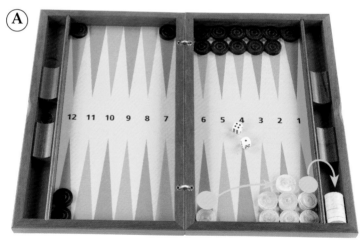

(**A**)

Bear with me (excuse the pun) while I explain this next "bearing off" rule. If you roll a number that is higher than any point occupied, a man from your **next highest** occupied point must be removed. The photograph (**B**) will make it easier for you to understand. In this example you rolled 5-2. The 2 is easy – just remove a man from W2. What about the 5? Your W5 and W6 points are unoccupied so you cannot bear off from W5 or make the move within your inner table. So the move is to bear off a man from W4 instead (**C**).

If you leave a blot while bearing off and your opponent hits it, the

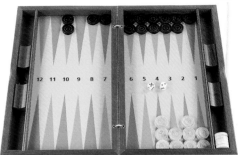

B

man goes to the bar and must be re-entered in your opponent's inner table, then brought all the way around the board again and into your own inner table before any further men can be borne off. Not nice!

C

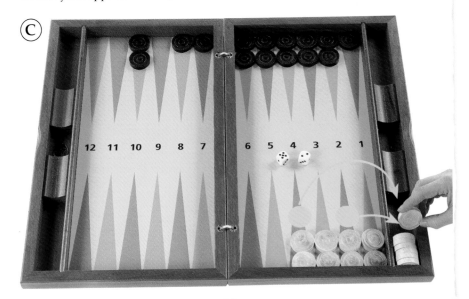

Starting the Game

YOU MUST always throw your dice in your right half of the board. Both dice must end up flat on the board, not on top of a man, on the bar or in the other half of the board. **Both** dice must be re-rolled if any of these infringements occur.

To start the game, each player rolls one die apiece (**A**). The person who throws the higher number gets to move first using his number and the number on his opponent's die. (If

you have both rolled the same number, the dice are re-thrown). So if you rolled a 5 and your opponent rolled a 3, your first move would be 5-3. When you have moved your two men, you pick up your die. Your opponent picks up his and then he rolls both of his own dice to discover what moves he can make. A move is only deemed completed when you pick up your dice from the board. If, in his excitement, your opponent rolls before you have picked up your dice, you can insist that he picks up his dice and re-rolls them.

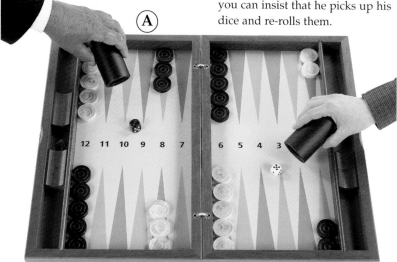

(A)

12 11 10 9 8 7   6 5 4 3

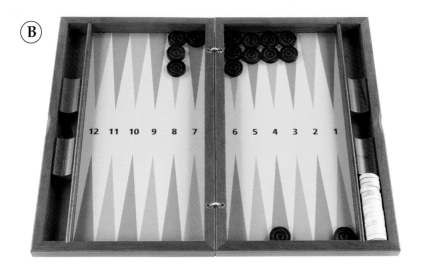

THREE WAYS TO WIN

You win a **single point game** when you have removed all 15 of your men before your opponent has removed all of his. He will, however, have removed at least one man.

You win a **gammon** or **double point game** when you have removed all 15 of your men before your opponent has removed any of his. However, all his men will be clear of your inner table.

You win a **backgammon** or **triple point game** if you have removed all 15 of your men and your opponent not only hasn't removed any of his, but he still has a man or men located in your inner table and/or on the bar (**B**).

THE DOUBLING CUBE

This is the fifth die in your set and it is considerably larger than the other four. The other difference is that it has numbers instead of spots. The six sides are numbered: 2, 4, 8, 16, 32 and 64 (**C**). I think it best if I come back to the subject of the doubling cube once I have taught you how to play the basic game (see pages 52-57). The cube is a gambling device and introduces an extra element of excitement into the proceedings. It should be treated with great respect – mastery of its subtleties definitely sorts out the sheep from the goats, the good players from the merely average.

The 36 Possible Throws

THERE ARE 36 different rolls that can be achieved by rolling the dice. To make this easy to explain, let us assume that you have one black die and one white die. Take, for example, the roll of 6-3. You could roll a 6 on the black die and a 3 on the white die. You could also roll a 6 on the white die and the 3 on the black die. So we see that there are two different ways to roll 6-3. Thus the odds that you will roll 6-3 are 2 in 36 rolls – or in gambling terms 17/1 against (two ways of throwing it and 34 ways of not throwing it = 34/2 or 17/1).

We can also see that there is only one way to roll doubles. So each double can only be rolled one way, giving odds of 35/1 against. The table that follows clearly illustrates the 36 possible rolls and the odds against throwing them (**A**).

The diagram opposite (**B**) is very revealing. It shows you at a glance

the odds against your opponent hitting any blot that you may have to leave. Its advice can be summed up by

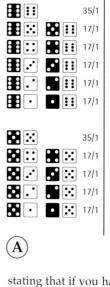

(A)

stating that if you have to leave a blot between one and six points away from the attacker, the **closer to him** you are the better. If you have to leave a blot between seven and 24 places away from the attacker, the **further away from him** you are the better. The only exception is 11 which is marginally safer than 12.

ODDS AGAINST HITTING A BLOT

DEGREE OF RISK... THESE ROLLS HIT

11 WAYS 25/1	12 WAYS 2/1	14 WAYS 11/7	15 WAYS 7/5	15 WAYS 7/5	17 WAYS 19/17	6 WAYS 5/1	6 WAYS 5/1	5 WAYS 31/5	3 WAYS 11/1	2 WAYS 17/1	3 WAYS 11/1	1 WAY 35/1	1 WAY 35/1	1 WAY 35/1	1 WAY 35/1	1 WAY 35/1
					6-5											
					6-4											
			4-6	5-6	6-3											
		3-6	4-5	5-4	6-2											
		3-5	4-3	5-3	6-1											
	2-6	3-4	4-2	5-2	1-6											
1-6	2-5	3-2	4-1	5-1	2-6											
1-5	2-4	3-1	1-4	1-5	3-6											
1-4	2-3	1-3	2-4	2-5	4-6											
1-3	2-1	2-3	3-4	3-5	5-6											
1-2	6-2	4-3	5-4	4-5	5-1											
6-1	5-2	5-3	6-4	6-5	1-5	6-1	6-2									
5-1	4-2	6-3	3-1	4-1	4-2	1-6	2-6	6-3								
4-1	3-2	2-1	1-3	1-4	2-4	5-2	5-3	3-6								
3-1	1-2	1-2	4-4	3-2	6-6	2-5	3-5	5-4	6-4		6-6					
2-1	2-2	3-3	2-2	2-3	3-3	4-3	4-4	4-5	4-6	6-5	4-4					
1-1	1-1	1-1	1-1	5-5	2-2	3-4	2-2	3-3	5-5	5-6	3-3	5-5	4-4	6-6	5-5	6-6
1	2	3	4	5	6	7	8	9	10	11	12	15	16	18	20	24

NUMBER OF POINTS THAT BLOT IS AWAY

(B)

You cannot be hit if you are 13, 14, 17, 19, 21, 22, or 23 points away from the attacker as there are no combinations of dice throws that add up to these totals.

General Strategy

A T THE start of any game,
certain strategic objectives
always apply. Like any good general,
however, you will have to learn to be
adaptable because the board layout
and your fortunes can change with
great rapidity. This is mainly due to
the factor of chance that is always
present in backgammon. No-one can
throw dice to order – especially when
they are shaken in and rolled from a
dice shaker.

The following objectives should
be your initial goals:

1) Get your two men that are in
Black's inner table on B1 clear and
away before they get blocked in.
2) Immediately start to build up a
row of blocked points ranging from
your W8 point down to your W3
point (**A**). The object is to contain
Black's two men that are in your
inner table on W1.
3) Strive to establish your 5 point and
your bar (7) point first.
4) If you get six blocked points in a
row (a prime) (**B**), Black will not be
able to escape. Even five, four or

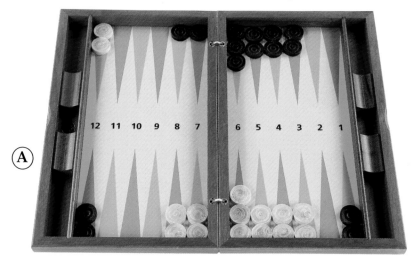

A

12 11 10 9 8 7   6 5 4 3 2 1

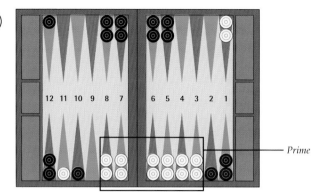

Prime

three blocked points (a semi-prime) will make his flight from your inner table more difficult.

5) If you are able to establish a six-point prime and Black has a man trapped on the wrong side of it, the prime should gradually be eased into your inner table – sending Black's man to the bar. This is called a **shutout** (C). Black must remain on the bar until, during the process of bearing off, you open up a point for him to re-enter on.

6) Where possible, move your pieces in pairs to avoid leaving unnecessary blots.

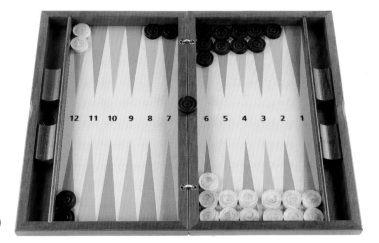

The Opening Moves

WHEN YOU first start to play you will find the opening sequences a little daunting. Don't panic – it is easier than it looks! Although no two games of backgammon are ever the same, the opening moves and replies to the opening moves have been thoroughly analyzed over the centuries and are nearly always played the same way.

The winner of the contest to see who will have the honour of starting first has 15 possible moves. This player has to use the value of the two dice that were rolled to establish who would start. As one die has to be higher than the other to achieve this, an opening roll of a double is impossible. The second player has the advantage of being able to throw a double which compensates them for the slight disadvantage of having to play second. The second player has 21 possible opening moves.

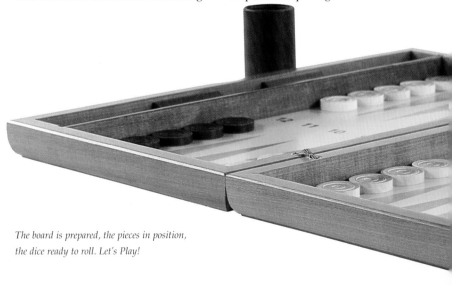

The board is prepared, the pieces in position, the dice ready to roll. Let's Play!

The best way to play them is explained below. I hasten to add that these are not the only ways to play the rolls. My recommendations are the best moves. All others are simply not as good.

ROLL	SUGGESTED PLAY		ROLL	SUGGESTED PLAY	
1-1	W6-W5 (2)	W8-W7 (2)	5-3	B12-W10	B12-W8
6-6	B1-B7 (2)	B12-W7 (2)	6-2	B12-W7	W7-W5
3-3	B1-B4 (2)	W8-W5 (2)	6-4	B1-B7	B7-B11
4-4	B1-B5 (2)	W8-W4 (2)	6-3	B1-B7	B7-B10
2-2	B12-W11 (2)	W6-W4 (2)	5-5	B12-W8 (2)	W8-W3 (2)
3-1	W8-W5	W6-W5	2-1	B12-W11	W6-W5
4-2	W8-W4	W6-W4	4-1	B12-W9	W6-W5
6-1	B12-W7	W8-W7	5-1	B12-W8	W6-W5
6-5	B1-B7	B7-B12	5-4	B12-W9	B12-W8
3-2	B12-W11	B12-W10	5-2	B12-W11	B12-W8
4-3	B12-W10	B12-W9			

We will briefly discuss each one. First let's look at the 15 openers.

The following pages illustrate my preferred opening moves. To understand why these are "preferred", you must remember the three main goals that you should try to achieve in the opening phase of play. Firstly, you want to build blocking points to contain your opponent's two back men. Secondly, you should aim to make an advanced point in your opponent's inner table – preferably his 5 point. Thirdly, you must try to achieve a flexible, well-balanced table that will give you the maximum potential to secure control of more points, and put you in a position to hit an opponent's blot if the opportunity arises.

3-1

One man from W8 to W5 and one man from W6 to W5 (**A**). This makes your 5 point. Control of the 5 points is important in backgammon – it certainly improves your chances of winning. A very strong opener.

4-2

W8 to W4 and W6 to W4 making your 4 point (**B**). You are on the way

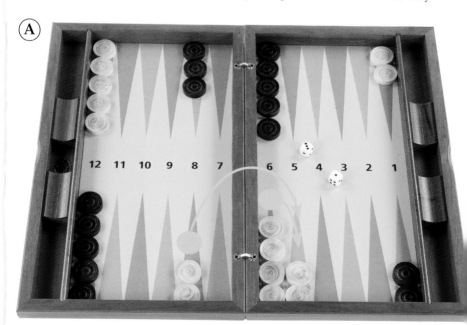

to building a prime that potentially may trap Black's two men at W1 in your inner table.

6-1
B12 to W7 and W8 to W7 making your 7 point (**C**). Backgammon players call this the "bar point". You now have three blocked points in a row, making Black's exit from your inner

table that much harder. He would need to throw 4-4 to get both men out on the next throw – that's a 35/1 shot. And if he doesn't, you will have a chance to build your prime.

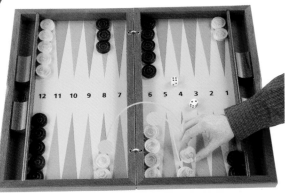

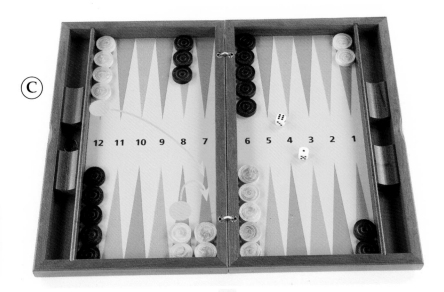

6-5

One man B1 to B7 then on to B12 (**A**). This is called "the Lovers Leap"! One of your men in Black's inner table has broken out and found a safe haven on B12.

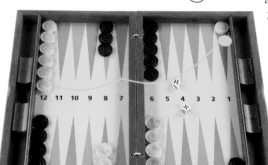

(**A**)

3-2

B12 to W11 and B12 to W10 (**B**). In their new positions the two men are ideally situated to help you form a prime. Agreed, you have left blots that Black might hit, but only a throw of 9 or 10 will hit them, and the odds against him throwing that are 31/5 against him throwing the 9 and 11/1 against throwing the 10.

4-3

B12 to W10 and B12 to W9 (**C**). Two "builders" to help you construct a prime. Again the blots are a long way from Black's men in your inner table, so they are relatively safe.

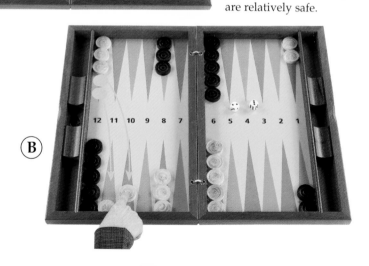

(**B**)

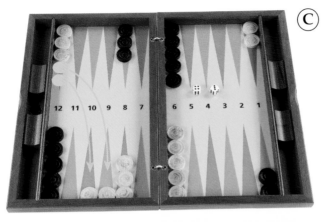

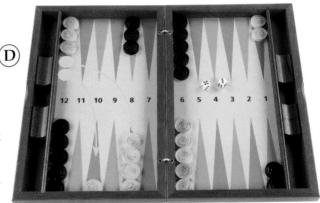

5-3

B12 to W10 and B12 to W8 (**D**) giving you two flexible "builders" that may well help you make your 5 or bar point on the next throw. Some experts recommend playing W8 to W3 and W6 to W3 thus making your 3 point. The move has merit but I think it is a mistake to go for such a forward blocked point so early in the game. You will now have to fill up the "hole" in your prime.

These first seven opening rolls are considered to be favourable. Count yourself lucky if you throw one of these. Over the page, I explain what to do if you have to play one of the eight other possible opening throws that are not as favourable to your chances.

The following eight rolls are considered to be unfavourable. My suggestions will help you to make the best out of a bad job!

6-2

B12 to W7 and W7 to W5 (**A**). This is a difficult roll to play. My suggestion leaves you with a blot on W5. Black may hit it with a 4 on his next roll – the table on page 17 shows us that 15 of the 36 possible rolls will hit it for odds of 7/5 against. You have to say to yourself: "What happens if he doesn't hit it?" Well – you are ideally positioned to block the point off on your next roll. Any 1, or 3 or 8 will do this – 24 possible closing rolls – that's 3/2 in your favour! Alternatively you may be able to use the man in conjunction with one of the others to make a point in your inner table.

6-4

B1 to B7 then B7 to B11 (**B**). You manage to free one of your back men from Black's inner table. Leaving it as a blot at B11 leaves it open to a 2 shot from Black. Only 11 rolls will hit it or, as an optimist might say, there are 25 rolls that will not hit it!

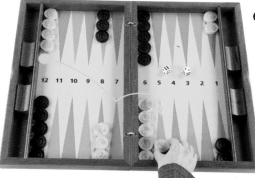

(**A**)

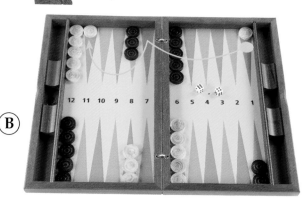

(**B**)

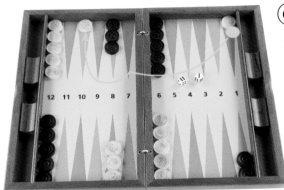

C

4-1

B12 to W9 and W6 to W5. We are again gambling that Black won't hit us. Our valuable bar and 5 points are quite easily made if he misses.

5-1

B12 to W8 and W6 to W5. Another positional gamble.

6-3

B1 to B7 and B7 to B10 (**C**). 23 rolls won't hit this blot!

5-4

B12 to W8 and B12 to W9. The W9 blot is only vulnerable to five rolls.

2-1

B12 to W11 and W6 to W5 (**D**). This play leaves two blots. There are 15 ways for Black to hit your blot at W5 and two ways to hit both the W5 and W11 blots. So Black has an almost evens chance of hitting one man and a 17/1 against chance of hitting both. What happens, however, if he misses? You are beautifully placed to make your bar point or 5 point on your next roll. It's a gamble. The alternative move B1 to B4 only weakens your defence.

5-2

B12 to W8 and B12 to W11. The W11 blot can only be hit two ways.

D

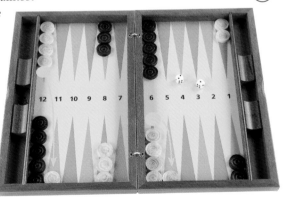

Replies to the Opening Moves

THE SECOND person to play has the advantage of the possibility of rolling doubles to start. There are six of them – five of which are extremely favourable. Here is how I suggest they should be played. (Note: the illustrations show Black's men in their starting position; in reality he will already have taken his move, and so the disposition of his men will be slightly different.)

1-1

This is the best opening roll. It should always be played two men from W6-W5 and two men from W8-W7 (**A**).

(**A**)

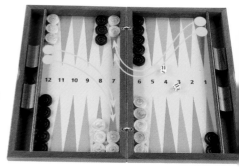

(**B**)

Although it leaves a blot at W8, it secures blocked points for you on W7 and W5, giving you a three-point semi-prime. Not bad for your first roll! On his next roll Black may hit your blot on W8 by rolling a 7. If you look back to the table on page 17 you will see that there are only six ways that he can do this. So the odds against him hitting the blot are 5/1. A gamble worth taking.

6-6

Move two men from B12 to W7 and two men from B1 to B7 (**B**). This secures your W7 point and

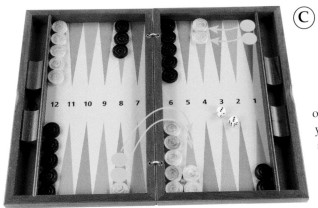

over-emphasized. If you can also subsequently get control of Black's 5, you will have a stranglehold on the entire game!

a three-point semi-prime and also brings your back men at B1 out of Black's inner table to the safety of B7. The position of these two men at B7 will greatly restrict Black's movements within the outer tables.

4-4

Move two men from B1 to B5 and two men from W8 to W4 (**D**). You make your 4 point but, what is much more important, you also occupy Black's 5 point!

3-3

Move two men from B1 to B4 and two men from W8 to W5 (**C**). You have advanced your back men to a more advantageous position from which to escape from Black's inner table. You have also secured your own 5 point. The importance of controlling the 5 points cannot be

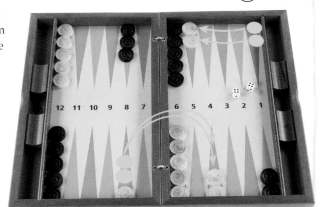

2-2

Play two men B12 to W11 and two men W6 to W4 (**A**). This makes your 4 point and brings two men down from B12 to help you in the process of building up a prime in future rolls.

5-5

Opening doubles are usually very useful. 5-5 is the exception. The play is two men from B12 to W8 then two men from W8 to W3 (**B**). This makes your 3 point. So, what is wrong with that? It is generally considered too early in the game to establish such an advanced point in your inner table. The result is a loss of flexibility in your prime-building aspirations.

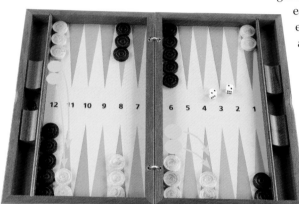

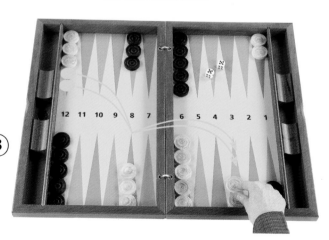

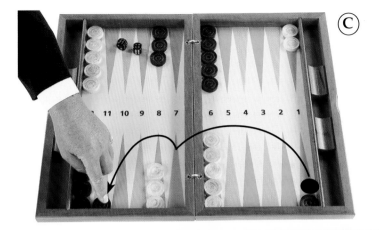

As the game has only just begun and the 30 men are still more or less in their starting positions you will find that most of the opening moves suggested on pages 22-29 will also still be relevant when you come to make your reply if Black has started the game. Common sense should always prevail; you must always keep your wits about you.

Suppose Black has won the toss, rolled 6-4 and played the classic opening move of running one man from W1 to W11 (C). You now roll 4-2. You should hit his blot with the 2 (D) and play the 4 elsewhere rather than make your W4 point.

It goes without saying that there are numerous exceptions to the rule and space does not permit me to go into them all here. Suffice it to say that in replying to the opening move, you must always carefully consider the consequences of your opponent's move first.

The Importance of Primes

A S I HAVE already stated one of your first objectives is to try to establish a prime or semi-prime.

The board position that is illustrated (**A**) shows White in possession of a full prime and Black with a semi-prime. White's aim will be to get his back men clear of Black's semi-prime as soon as possible. At the same time he will try to ease his full prime further into his inner table by using his other three men – leapfrogging them over the prime – to make a point on W3 and still keep

his prime intact. Having made the W3 point, he will now attempt to make the W2 point. Black is trapped.

How should Black play this situation? He will try to cause White to break up his prime while at the same time increasing his own semi-prime into a full one, thus keeping White's two back men firmly imprisoned. He will also attempt to make the W3 point, so punching White's prime on the nose and preventing it from sliding further into the inner board.

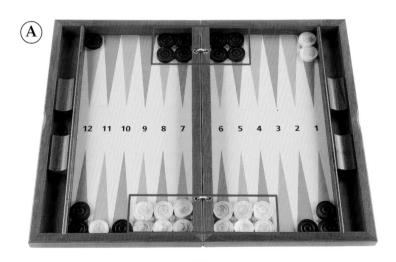

12 11 10 9 8 7   6 5 4 3 2 1

(B)

THE SHUTOUT

This photograph (**B**) illustrates a **shutout prime**. Black has a man on the bar and cannot re-enter. Until he does, he is unable to move any of his other pieces. White can just keep on rolling and moving until he has to open an inner table point while bearing off, or because no other course is open to him. Black must then attempt to re-enter from the bar and rush home as fast as he can to try to save the game.

THE BLOCKING GAME

We have discussed primes and semi-primes. Using this technique is called playing a blocking game. It is best to opt for this style of play if you manage to establish your 5 and bar points early on in the game. You should then attempt to increase the width of your semi-prime into a full six-point prime. Then slide it slowly but surely into your inner table to prevent your opponent from escaping from your clutches.

Playing Against a Prime

OCCASIONALLY YOU will encounter a situation where both players have a full prime in operation (**A**). Please study the illustration carefully. Who do you think will win? Black is farther advanced than White, but in this position White is the favorite to win. If White slows his play down as much as possible, Black will have to break up his prime first, so allowing White's back man on B1 to escape.

White should avoid the temptation of hitting Black's blot on W1 at all costs. Hitting it would enable Black to keep his prime intact while trying to re-enter. You as White should attempt to make the W4 point by throwing a spare man ahead of the prime at W4 (**B**) and then covering it

(**A**)

12 11 10 9 8 7 6 5 4 3 2 1

with another man from W10 or W8 if you haven't already used the third man from this point (**C**). Make W3 in the same way – then W2. Don't worry if Black hits one of your blots. He will have to break up his prime while you are re-entering or waiting to re-enter from the bar.

By the time you have advanced your prime to W2, Black should have had to break up his prime and your man on B1 can escape. Now you can hit his blot on W1 and create a shutout prime!

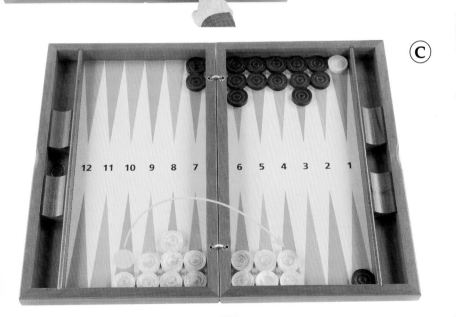

B

C

The Running Game

ALL BACKGAMMON games eventually end up as "running games." This is the state of play where no more contact exists between the opposing forces and it is now one mad rush to see who can bear off first. Although extremely unlikely, it is possible to find yourself in a running game after only two rolls each. If both players rolled 6-5 twice and chose to run both their back men with "lovers leaps," the board would look like (**A**).

Usually it takes quite a few rolls before a running game situation emerges. Here is a typical layout (**B**). White has rolled 5-4 and chosen to move B12 to W8 and B12 to W9 (**C**). He saw that by this move he would put himself two rolls ahead of Black, so he decided to dash for home! Now, providing that Black doesn't throw doubles every time White should win comfortably. How did White know it was time to run? The explanation is over the page!

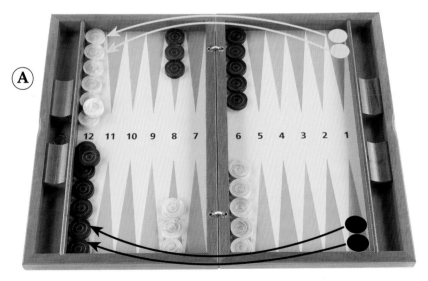

(**A**)

(B)

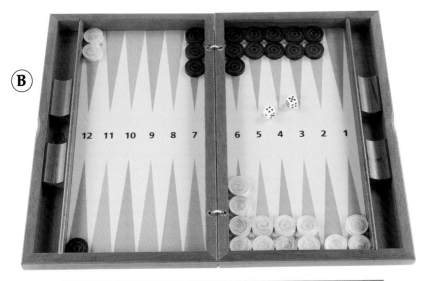

12 11 10 9 8 7   6 5 4 3 2 1

(C)

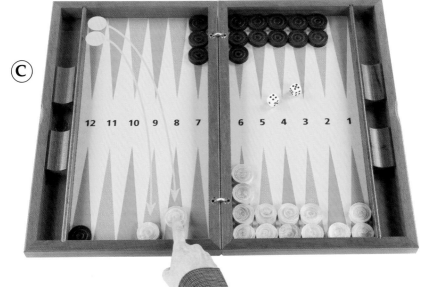

12 11 10 9 8 7   6 5 4 3 2 1

Calculating Your Position

THE RELATIVE positions of the two players can be assessed at any given moment in the game. The average total of the two dice that you throw is $8\frac{1}{6}$. (For calculation purposes we will round it down to 8.) This means that your board will advance by an average of 8 points each throw. With this in mind we have to work out how many throws each player is likely to need to bear off all of his men. The two totals are subtracted, one from the other, and the result is the number of throws one player is ahead of the other.

It sounds complicated but don't panic! I have devised a very easy way to do this. Look at the diagrams (**A**) and (**B**). One is a grid to calculate White's position (**A**), and the other is a grid to calculate Black's position. Now superimpose the grids over the white and black men shown in the board positions on page 37 (**C**) (**D**).

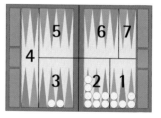

(C)

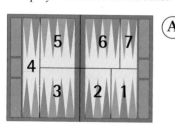

(A)

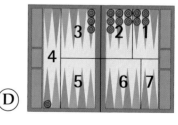

(D)

(B)

Let's look at White's position first. Each man is given the value of the sector that it is in. White has five men in the 1 sector = 5; eight men in the 2 sector: 8 x 2 =16; and two men in the

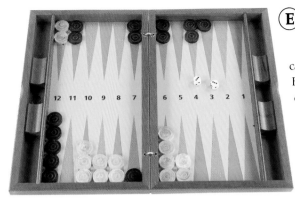

(E)

calculation reveals that Black scores 49 and White only 41. So White is already four rolls ahead! Hitting Black's blot is unnecessary and should be avoided at all costs. White should opt for a running game by playing the two men from B12 to W10 and two men from W6 to W3 (**F**). This reduces White's score to 37. That is a full six rolls ahead! Barring a heart attack, White will now win hands down!

Note: Any man that sits on the bar is counted as a 7.

3 sector: 2 x 3 = 6. So White's score is 5+16+6 = 27.

Black has got four men in his 1 sector = 4; seven men in his 2 sector: 7 x 2 = 14; three men in his 3 sector: 3 x 3 = 9; and one man in his 4 sector = 4. Black's score is 4+14+9+4 = 31.

The difference between the two scores is four. Four what? The value of four dice or, in other words, White is **two complete rolls ahead** of Black. All you do is calculate the two scores, subtract one from the other, and divide the answer by two. Easy!

Look at the next illustration (**E**). White has just rolled 3-3. Should he hit Black's blot on W7? A quick

(F)

The Back Game

T HIS IS an interesting strategy and one that you should study carefully. It can sometimes save a "lost" game for you. I say "sometimes" because the odds of you pulling it off are less than even. However, often you have no choice. Don't get involved in a back game unless you have no other option.

In a back game you attempt to get all your men off first, yet seem to be leaving blots all over the place for your opponent to hit! Suppose that, in the early stages of the game, you have been hit twice and now find that you have four back men in Black's inner table controlling two points. To add insult to injury, Black's two back men have escaped from W1. Your position might look something like this (**A**). Things look pretty hopeless.

(**A**)

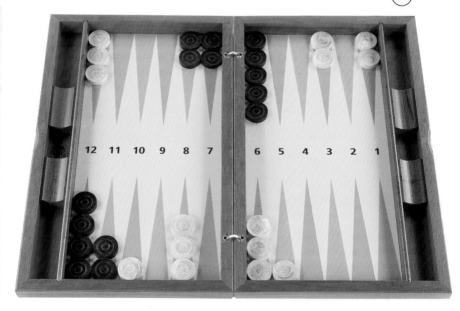

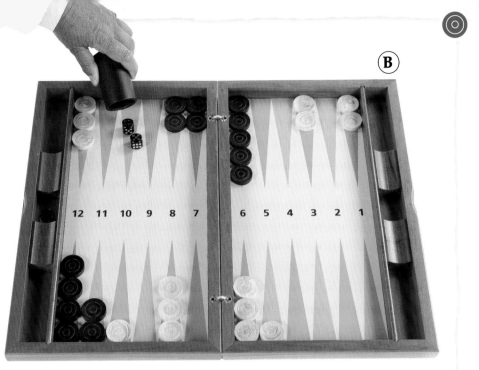

The only way for you to win is to hit a Black blot or two and at the same time build up a prime or even a shutout for the blot to sit behind. There is no guarantee that you will hit a blot even if you are offered one. It is a chancy business. Your worst enemy in playing a back game is **timing**. High rolls will cause you to advance too quickly and have to break up the two points that you control in Black's inner table. The two points that you control make it extremely difficult for Black to bring

all of his pieces in safely – so he may have to leave you a blot to aim at. For example, if Black should roll 5-4 in this position (**B**) he has to leave a blot somewhere.

You need to control at least two points in his inner table to have any chance of success. The B1 and B3 points are the best. In descending order, the points of preference that you should control are: 1 and 3; 1 and 2; 2 and 3; 2 and 4; 3 and 4; 1 and 4; 3 and 5; 4 and 5. Any other combinations are pretty useless.

If you are very behind and have three men back in Black's inner table, you should open up your position and try to get him to hit a blot. Then you can re-enter a fourth man into Black's inner table and possibly close off the second point. The photograph (**A**) illustrates a most unfavorable position for White. Apart from having a dreadful position, he is also two rolls behind. Black controls White's 5 point and also has a useful semi-prime holding up White's three back men.

White rolls 2-1. What should he do? Should he play W11 to W9 – making the W9 point – and W7 to W6, tidying things up somewhat? No! The correct play for White's 2-1 here would be B9 to B10 and B1 to B3 (**B**)!

White moves to B11 giving Black five blots to aim at in the outer tables. He also plays B1 to B3 to stake a claim on Black's 3 point. If Black now hits a blot it will have to be re-entered. Hopefully White will roll a 3 thus securing the point. A back game would then be a possibility.

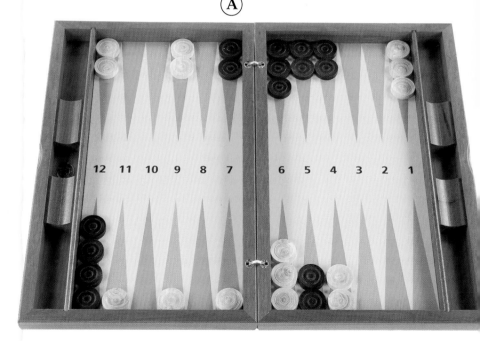

(**A**)

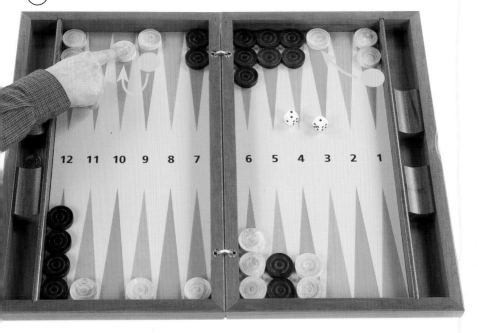

12 11 10 9 8 7   6 5 4 3 2 1

If Black is an experienced player he will do everything he can to avoid hitting a blot – although in this example he will be hard pushed not to do so.

PLAYING AGAINST A BACK GAME

So what have we learned from this section? If you are playing against a back game:

• Try not to give your opponent more than three back men to play with.

• Try to speed up his advancement.
• Play very carefully and don't take any unnecessary chances.
• Be extremely careful bringing your men into your inner table and bearing them off. Play the "percentage" move every time.

Here is a sobering thought for you: even if you have borne off 14 of your 15 men, it is still possible for you to lose the game. Possible but not very probable!

Bearing Off

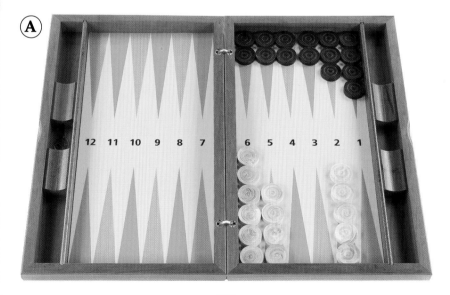

M ANY GAMES are lost unnecessarily by making wrong moves during the process of bearing your men off. You must take great care during the process of bringing your men into your inner table in the endgame.

Costly Gaps And Overloaded Points

Try to achieve as balanced an inner table as possible. Look at the

illustration (**A**). White has no men on his W1, W3, and W4 points. This means that the move for any 1, 3, or 4 that he rolls will have to be made within his inner table. He will not be able to bear men off for a 1, 3, or 4 throw as things stand. This could set White back a roll or two. Look at Black's beautifully balanced inner table. A position count (**B**) (**C**) shows White as 25 and Black as 21. So White is already two rolls behind! Add to

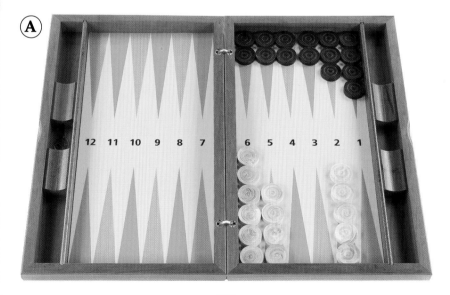

(A)

12	11	10	9	8	7		6	5	4	3	2	1

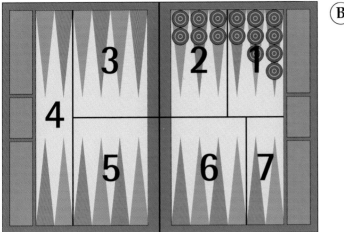

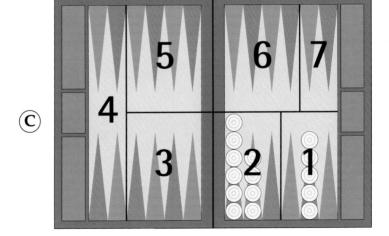

C

this the near certainty that he will have to make at least a couple of internal moves within his inner table puts White in an untenable situation.

Of course, White *could* actually clear his board in four rolls by rolling a sequence of doubles: 6-6, 6-6, 5-5, and 2-2. And pigs might fly!

High or Low—First or Last

L OOK AT this illustration (**A**) carefully. It is White's move and he has rolled 5-3. How should he play it? The following illustrations show three different ways to play the move. Here (**B**) White bears a man off from W5 and another man from W3. This is a thoughtless move because it leaves a blot on W3 for Black to aim at. Look at Black's closed inner table! If Black now rolls a 2, White will almost certainly lose the game because White's man will have to remain on the bar while Black brings the rest of his men around and starts to bear off.

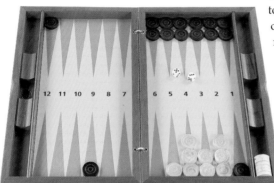

A

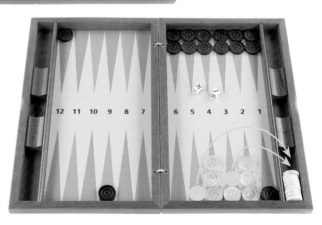

B

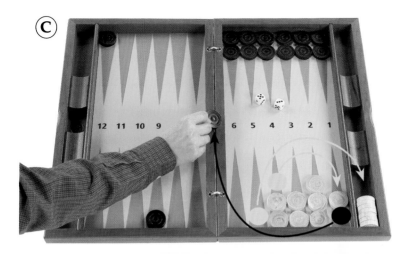

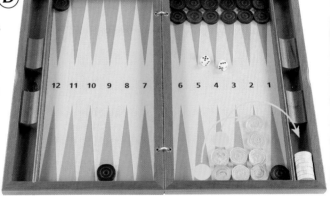

Now look at this one (**C**). This is another disaster! White has borne off a man at W5 for the 5, and played W4 to W1 for the 3, hitting Black's blot and sending it to the bar. If Black now rolls a 1, White's game could well be lost.

The correct play for this 5-3 roll is shown here (**D**). White first plays W5 to W2 for the 3 and secondly bears off one man from W4 for the 5!

The rules of backgammon state

that you must play both halves of your roll if at all possible. It is immaterial which half of the roll you play first. By playing the smaller number first, White is able to avoid leaving a blot.

Which One First?

LOOK AT this position (**A**). It is White's roll. White has a total of six men on his W6 and W5 points. An even number. Only three rolls can cause White a problem forcing him to leave a blot for Black to aim at: 4-4, 4-6, and 6-4. That makes three out of 36 possible rolls or 11/1 against it happening.

In the next position (**B**) just one man has been moved so that White now has a total of five men on his W6 and W5 points. An uneven number. Now there are six horror rolls for White – twice as many as in the previous example! They are: 6-6 (**C**), 4-4, 6-5, 5-6, 5-3, and 3-5. There is a 5/1 chance that White will leave a blot.

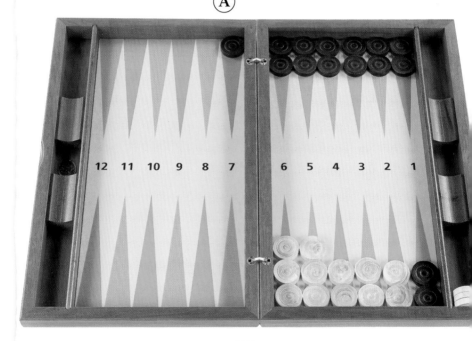

(**A**)

| 12 | 11 | 10 | 9 | 8 | 7 | | 6 | 5 | 4 | 3 | 2 | 1 |

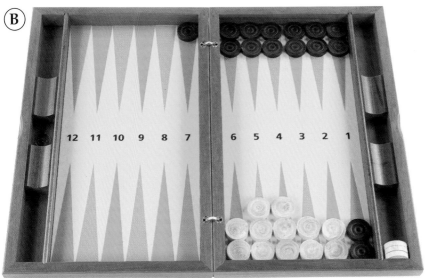

The rule to remember, therefore, is:

• Whenever possible you should leave an even number of men on your highest two points when bearing off.

49

The Odds

BACKGAMMON IS at heart a gambling game and I advise you always to play for some stake or other – even if it is only matches, or a penny a game. It is surprising how fast you can learn to play well if your mistakes are costing you something!

Good players are always looking ahead. They say to themselves: "What would happen if I move a man to this point? What are the odds that my opponent will hit me if I leave a blot here. Would it be more advantageous if I left a blot here instead?" Every possible alternative move is considered, evaluated and the best move then chosen. The "percentage" roll is played.

We know that there are only 36 possible rolls, and the odds of throwing any specific roll have been explained on pages 16-17. Try to commit these figures to memory. This is essential information if you aspire to become a good player. The ability to calculate the true odds and to work out the relative positions of the two players will be an invaluable asset when you begin to play games using the doubling cube. If you are offered

the doubling cube and you accept it, you are effectively playing for double the original stake money – so your assessment of the situation and the true odds is vital.

THE ODDS FOR AND AGAINST RE-ENTERING FROM THE BAR

Here is more useful information, and again I have done the mathematical donkey work for you. The first table (A) shows the odds for and against re-entering one man from the bar depending on the number of open points available.

NUMBER OF OPEN POINTS	WAYS TO COME IN	% CHANCE OF RE-ENTERING	ODDS FOR OR AGAINST
5	35	97%	35/1 in favour
4	32	89%	8/1 in favour
3	27	75%	3/1 in favour
2	20	56%	5/4 in favour
1	11	31%	25/11 against

NUMBER OF OPEN POINTS	WAYS TO COME IN	% CHANCE OF RE-ENTERING	ODDS FOR OR AGAINST
5	25	69%	25/11 in favour
4	16	44%	5/4 against
3	9	25%	3/1 against
2	4	11%	8/1 against
1	1	2.7%	35/1 against

(B)

The next table (**B**) shows the odds for and against re-entering two men from the bar.

ODDS FOR AND AGAINST BEARING OFF

The odds for and against bearing off your last man or last two men in one or two rolls are shown in the third table (**C**). The doubling cube really comes into its own during endgame bearing-off contests, so it is vitally important that you are aware of your true position.

POINTS ON WHICH MAN OR MEN ARE LOCATED	NUMBER OF WAYS TO BEAR ALL OFF FIRST TIME	ODDS IN FAVOUR OR AGAINST	YOUR % PROBABILITY OF BEARING ALL OFF IN TWO ROLLS
6 and 6	4	8/1 against	78%
6 and 5	6	5/1 against	88%
5 and 5	6	5/1 against	92%
6 and 4	8	7/2 against	93%
5 and 4	10	13/5 against	96%
6 and 3	10	13/5 against	97%
4 and 4	11	25/11 against	98%
6 and 2	13	23/13 against	99%
5 and 3	14	11/7 against	99%
6 and 1	15	7/5 against	99+%
4 and 3	17	19/17 against	99+%
3 and 3	17	19/17 against	99+%
5 and 2	19	19/17 in favour	100% certain
5 and 1	23	23/13 in favour	100% certain
4 and 2	23	23/13 in favour	100% certain
3 and 2	25	25/11 in favour	100% certain
2 and 2	26	13/5 in favour	100% certain
6	27	3/1 in favour	100% certain
4 and 1	29	29/7 in favour	100% certain
5	31	31/5 in favour	100% certain
3 and 1	34	17/1 in favour	100% certain
4	34	17/1 in favour	100% certain
2 and 1	36	Certain to bear off	100% certain
3	36	Certain to bear off	100% certain
1 and 1	36	Certain to bear off	100% certain
2	36	Certain to bear off	100% certain

(C)

The Doubling Cube

IF YOU have managed to read through the book thus far you will now be able to play backgammon – after a fashion! The game has been played for centuries and the general rules can be learned by almost anybody in 20 minutes. Because of its heady mix of strategy plus the unpredictable element of chance, it remains a superb two-person board game. To learn to play the game well, however, is a different matter. You could spend a lifetime studying the nuances and subtleties of the game.

In the 1920s an unknown player in New York introduced the doubling cube into the game. This revolutionized backgammon and transformed it from being just a good game into the best, most exciting two-person board game in the world. The cube (as backgammon players call it) should be treated with great respect at all times. It has the power of sorting out the men from the boys!

How The Cube Is Used

The cube is shaped like a die (**A**). Its six sides are numbered 2, 4, 8, 16, 32 and 64. At the start of the game the

(A)

cube is placed on the centre of the bar with the number 64 uppermost. At this stage it belongs to no one (**B**).

If during the course of the game you feel that your position is stronger than your opponents, before you roll your dice you can, if you wish, pick up the cube, turn it so that the number 2 is uppermost and place it on the board directly in front of your opponent (**C**). This action is saying to your opponent that you think you will win and you wish to continue to play but from this moment on you wish to double the stake money. If you had arranged to play for £1 a game, you now wish to play for £2.

Your opponent has two options:

1) He can agree to the increased stake money. He signifies this acceptance

52

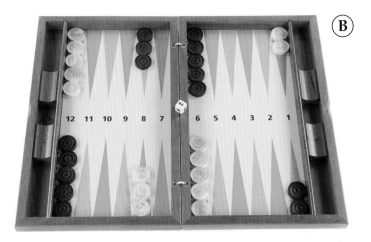

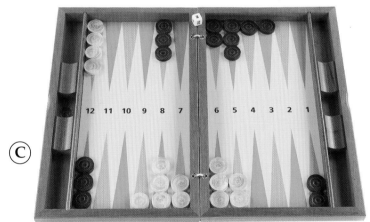

by picking up the cube and placing it on the bar on his side of the board still with the number 2 showing. Play continues for a £2 stake per game. He now "owns" the cube and only he can re-double.

2) He can refuse to accept the increased stake. In this case the game ends right there and he has to pay you the original £1 stake. The pieces are all reset and a new game commences for another £1 stake.

You will find that fortunes can fluctuate dramatically in backgammon. After a few more rolls your opponent may feel that the positions have been reversed and that he now holds the upper hand. He can now re-double you. He places the cube in front of you with the 4 uppermost (**A**). If you accept it you control the cube and are now playing for £4 a game! Refusal by you will cost you £2 and a new game is automatically started.

Theoretically the cube can bat backwards and forwards and in no time at all you could find yourself playing for £64 in a game that started out with a £1 wager! That £64 will also be multiplied by the way you win or lose. A **gammon** is a 2-point

game and would cost the loser £64 x 2 = £128. If the loser is **backgammoned**, which is a 3-point game, the debt will be a hefty £64 x 3 = £192! Wow!

When two players are evenly matched and sensible play prevails, the cube will very seldom go over 8.

I would recommend that you restrict the cube to 8 by prior arrangement. This could still cost you £24 or matchsticks or peanuts – whatever you are using as currency.

AUTOMATIC DOUBLES
It is a common practice in backgammon circles to turn the cube to 2 if you both throw the same number when you are choosing who plays first. The cube is then left on

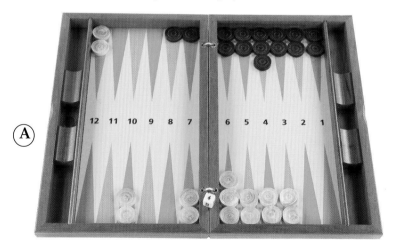

(**A**)

the centre of the bar and either player can make the first re-double. I must stress that automatic doubles can only be made by prior arrangement. So set the ground rules before you start your backgammon session to avoid any arguments later.

Some groups even play two automatic doubles – the cube going to 4 if both players again throw a tie. I would strongly discourage this because I feel that it ruins the game. Even a single game will cost the loser a minimum of four points. This will take some clawing back.

BEAVERS

A beaver is an instant re-double. This rule can only be played by mutual consent. It is frowned upon in tournament play. It can, however, act as a powerful psychological tool if you feel that your opponent has offered you an unsound double.

If you feel very strongly that he has made a bad mistake in offering you a double, you accept the cube with a smile, turn it from 2 to 4 and place it on the bar on your own side (B) saying "I beaver you!"

What you are saying is that you think he is crazy and should see a psychiatrist! You are so sure that he is mistaken, you are willing to play on for twice the amount that he was suggesting. If he accepts the beaver you play on for £4 a point. The subtle difference from a conventional re-double is that you still control the cube. If he refuses the beaver, he must pay you the £2 and once again a new game is started.

General Doubling Advice

IT IS very important that you learn to use the cube well and wisely. It is a difficult art. So many things have to be taken into consideration:

• What is your position?
• Is your opponent easily bluffed?
• Does he accept doubles without considering his position?
• Does it look likely that you will win a gammon or backgammon?

You would be silly to offer the cube in this instance because you would be giving him the opportunity to refuse, thus bringing the game to a shuddering halt. You will have thrown away a two-, or possibly even a three-point win.

I never double early. A favourable doubling situation exists when:

• My opponent has two or three (not four) back men.
• I have established a semi-prime of at least four points.
• I am at least two or three rolls better off than my opponent.
• My opponent is not in a position to mount a back game because his timing is wrong.

I always double in a running game if I am two or more rolls ahead. This is an insurance against my opponent throwing a whole string of doubles. Given equal luck, I am as likely to throw as many doubles as he does – but anything can happen in this wicked game!

SHOULD YOU ACCEPT A DOUBLE?
Your decision to accept a double or re-double should be based only on your chances of winning and **not** the amount of money that is staked. If it is correct for you to accept a double at 2, it is just as valid to accept it at 16!

Your second consideration should be to accept any double where you find yourself no more than a 3/1 underdog! This is a simple mathematical fact. Odds of 3/1 against you means that in similar situations you will lose three out of every four times. If you refuse all four situations you will lose say £4. If you accept all four you are likely to lose three of them (-6) and win one (+2) which gives a loss of £4 – exactly the same situation as if you had refused all four.

Your "plus" is the fact that the tide may turn in your favour and you may manage to defy the odds – it is a game of chance after all! You could win a couple of the games and thus break even.

If you are a 2/1 underdog and refuse the double in all three situations you will lose £3. If at 2/1 against you accept all three, you stand to lose two games for a £4 loss and win one for a gain of £2. Your net loss would be only £2, which is a £1 better off than you would have been if you had refused all three!

These are the purely mathematical facts regarding the offering or acceptance of a double. Evaluating your position in an endgame is relatively simple. You can quite easily work out the possible outcome of the next one, two or three moves and the odds for or against you winning.

However, it is almost impossible to calculate the exact odds of winning or losing in a mid-game situation. I suggest that you look for the following indicators before offering a double:

• You should have two or three (no more) of his men trapped in your inner table.
• You should have a prime or strong semi-prime made up of consecutive points.
• You should have no more than one of your own men blocked in his inner table.
• You should be at least two or three rolls ahead of your opponent in a position count.

Personally, I accept all early doubles but never offer them. I only offer a double if I think my opponent should refuse to accept it.

Playing Etiquette

I CAN ALWAYS recognize good backgammon players. They have an "air" about them. They appear to be supremely confident. Not arrogant – just totally relaxed. They cleverly try to disguise their skill. They all have one thing in common – the will to win. To come second in a game of backgammon is to lose. If an expert loses, he tends to think of it as a miscarriage of justice! To them, attitude is everything.

If an expert chess player is matched against an inexperienced player, the expert will win every time. Not so in backgammon. Because the dice introduce a chance element into the otherwise skilful strategic game, upsets can and regularly do happen. An expert will probably beat a novice four out of every five times. It is this fifth time that makes the game so exciting to play and encourages the novice to improve.

TOP TEN HINTS
1. Never be frightened to play **anyone**.
2. Only play for the amount of money that you can afford to lose.

3. Set the terms of play before you start. How many doubles? What about automatic doubles? Can you beaver?
4. Appreciate your opponent's good play but don't show it!
5. Don't show your annoyance to your opponent however bad your luck may seem to be.
6. Don't count out your move by tapping the man on each point. This action will immediately signal to your opponent that you are a beginner. The board is laid out in order to help you count. All the diagonally opposite points in the outer or inner tables are a count of six points away from each other (**A**). The internal dimension of each table is a count of five, while

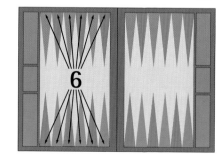

(**A**)

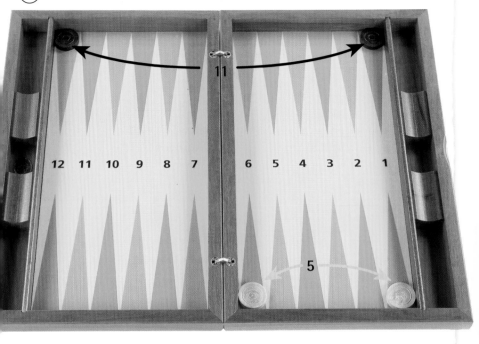

the full span of one side of the board – i.e. from B1 to B12 – is a count of eleven (**B**). In most backgammon sets the points are marked in alternating colours. If you roll an even number you will end up on a pointer of the same colour as the one your man is presently sitting on. If you roll an odd number you will end up on a pointer of the other colour.

7. Learn to play at a reasonable pace – try to establish a rhythm that is neither too fast nor too slow.

8. Be comfortable when you play. A good chair and a well-lit board are important.

9. Once you have thrown, work out the move that you intend to make in your head. Once you "see" it, make your move in a positive way.

10. Learn the official rules of backgammon (see pages 60-61). Get them off pat so that you can quote them in cases of dispute. Stick to the official rules and make sure that your opponents do too.

The Official Rules of Backgammon

T HESE RULES came into
operation in 1931 and have been
adopted by clubs and players
throughout the world. It will be in
your interest to learn then thoroughly,
but quote them only if a
procedural dispute arises. **(A)**

THE GAME

1. The game of Backgammon is
played by two persons.
2. Thirty men, fifteen of one colour
and fifteen of another are set out as
shown (**A**) on a standard board of
four quarters or tables each having

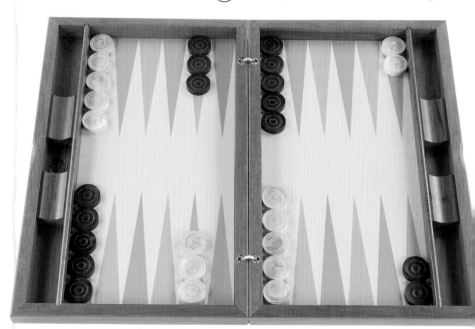

six points. In the illustration the player's inner tables are shown to the right. This means that White's inner table is opposite his right hand, and Black's inner table is opposite his left hand. In actual play it is customary to have the inner tables nearest the light.

3. For entering and bearing off, the points in both inner tables are considered as numbered from one to six, beginning with the point nearest the edge of the board.

4. Direction of play is from the opponent's inner table to the opponent's outer table, to your outer table, and then to your own inner table.

5. Two dice, thrown from a cup in which the dice are shaken before being thrown govern play of the men.

6. For the first game either player may ask to roll for choice of seats, men, or dice. Alternatively they may just sit down, set up and play.

7. At the start of any later game either player may ask to mix the dice. In this case he shakes the four dice together in one cup and rolls them out. The opponent selects a die, then the roller, then the opponent, with the roller taking the last one.

THE THROWS

8. For the opening throw, each player throws a single die. A tie requires another opening throw. Whoever throws the highest number wins, and for his first move plays the numbers upon both dice. After that each player in turn throws two dice.

9. The dice must be shaken thoroughly, rolled together, and come to rest flat (i.e. not "cocked") upon the table to the players right. Otherwise they must be thrown again.

10. There must be a re-throw if a throw is made before the opponent's play is completed.

11. A play is deemed completed when a player has moved his men and starts to pick up his dice. If he starts to pick them up before playing all numbers he is legally allowed to, his opponent has the right to compel him to complete or not to complete his play. A roll by his opponent is considered an acceptance of the play as made. (See Rule 20).

THE PLAY

12. The play of the men consists of:

(a) Moving a man (or men) the exact number of points indicated by the number on each of the two dice thrown. One man may be moved the total of the two dice, or one man may be moved the number shown on one die, and an entirely different man the number shown on the other die.

(b) Entering a man from the bar, in the opponent's inner table, on a point corresponding to the number on a die thrown.

(c) Bearing off a man in the player's inner table, when no man is left outside that table or on the bar, in accordance with Rule 18.

13. Doubles require four plays of the number on the dice.

14. Plays must be made for both dice if possible. Either number may be played first. If either number may be played, but not both, then the highest number must be played.

15. No play may be made which lands, or touches down, on a point held by two or more of the opponent's men.

16. When a play lands on a point occupied by a single man (blot) of the opponent's, such a man is "hit" and must be lifted from the board by the hitter and placed on the bar in the centre of the playing board, to await entry in accordance with Rule 12(b).

17. A player having a man on the bar may not play any other man until that man has been re-entered.

18. When in a position to bear off,

you may bear off a man from a point corresponding to the number on a die thrown, or from the highest occupied point which is lower than the number indicated by a die. If a number is thrown for an unoccupied point, no man below can be borne off using this number, while any man remains on a higher point. You are not required to bear off a man if you are able and prefer to move forward on the board. Rule 14 applies here as in all other situations.

Errors

19. If an error has been made in the set-up, it must be corrected if either player notices it before the second play of a game has been completed.

20. If an error in play has been made, either player may require it to be corrected before a subsequent throw, but not thereafter. The man played in error must be correctly played if possible. You are not obliged to point out an opponent's error if it is to your advantage to ignore it.

Scoring

21. The player who first bears off all of his men wins a game. A gammon (double game) is won if the opponent has not borne off a single man. A backgammon (triple game) is won if the opponent has not borne off a single man and has one or more men still in the winner's inner table or upon the bar. This triples the count for a single game.

22. The count is raised (i.e. the doubling cube comes into play):

(a) *Automatically*: Each tie that occurs on the opening throw of a game doubles the previous count. However, these automatic doubles are not played unless both players have previously agreed to use them and an understanding has been reached as to the method and limitations of such doubles.

(b) *Voluntarily*: Either player may offer the first double of the previous count. After that the right to double the previous count alternates, being always with the player who accepted the last double.

A double or re-double may be offered only when it is the player's turn to play and before he has thrown the dice. He shall be deemed to have thrown the dice even if he rolls cocked dice. A double may be accepted or declined. The refusal of a double terminates the game, and the player refusing loses whatever the count may amount to before the double was offered.

23. Gammons and backgammons double and treble the last doubling count respectively.

Chouette

CHOUETTE IS a social form of backgammon. Let us suppose that there are five people in your group. Each of you rolls a die (ties are re-rolled) so that you end up with a playing order from the highest to the lowest. The highest roller becomes "the man in the box" and sits on one side of the board. The other four players take him on! The second highest roller becomes the Captain and sits opposite the man in the box. The game proceeds in the normal way except that the Captain (who alone moves the pieces) can confer with his team members before committing his team to the move that he suggests. The other team members can confer and offer advice to the Captain if they think he is not making the best move. The Captain's decision, however, is final.

If the man in the box wins the game, he collects the appropriate amount from each player in the team! The Captain is then demoted to the end of the line and the next member of the team becomes the Captain.

If the man in the box loses – then he has to pay out to each member of the team. He now goes to the end of the team. The Captain now changes sides and becomes the man in the box. The highest-ranking member of the team becomes the new Captain and a new game commences.